Caucasus Mts.

PONTUS EUXINUS
(BLACK SEA)

Odessus

Apollonia

MACEDONIA

ASIA MINOR

IONIAN SEA

RIA

SEA

cuse

CRETE

CYPRUS

Sidon
Tyre

S Y R I A

A N E A N   S E A

CYRENAICA

Libyan

Desert

E G Y P T

Nile River

RED SEA

MAN &
ANCIENT
CIVILIZATIONS

Also by Carla Greene:

Our Living Earth
How Man Began
Before the Dinosaurs
After the Dinosaurs
How to Know Dinosaurs

MAN & ANCIENT CIVILIZATIONS

by Carla Greene

illustrations by Marika

the bobbs-merrill company inc.

indianapolis   new york

Library of Congress Cataloging in Publication Data

Greene, Carla.
   Man and ancient civilizations.

   SUMMARY: Discusses the culture, science, industry, and government of ancient civilizations from the Neolithic Age through the Golden Age of Greece and
Rome. Includes those of the Sumerians, Assyrians, Hittites, Babylonians, Hebrews, Phoenicians, and Egyptians.
   1. Civilizations, Ancient—Juvenile literature. [1. Civilizations, Ancient] I. Title.
CB311.G685   930   76-47339
ISBN 0-672-52251-9

CONTENTS

CIVILIZATION BEGINS

In its original meaning, the word civilization referred merely to people "living in cities" as opposed to those living in unpopulated or wilderness areas. But the meaning of the word has become much broader. When we speak of ancient civilizations, we refer to large groups of people not only living in cities but having an organized form of government and a high level of culture, science, industry, and creative arts.

Civilizations, in this sense, already existed in many parts of the world about 5,000 years ago. The greatest of these civilizations and the ones having the most influence on the Western world developed and prospered in the Middle East. These consisted of Mesopotamia (the land of the

Bible), Ancient Egypt, Ancient Greece, the Ancient Persian Empire, and Ancient Rome.

We know about these great civilizations through the work of scientists called *archeologists* who devote themselves to digging up evidences of the past. Their excavations have brought to light examples of ancient pottery, primitive tools, jewelry, sculpture, paintings, and even whole cities dating back thousands of years. They study and analyze their discoveries, determining the age of each item and the kind of civilization it represents. Putting these together with written records which have existed for the past 5,000 years, they can determine the culture, art, science, and religion of the civilizations existing during a particular period.

In this book you will find out a great deal about these important Middle East civilizations. You will probably wonder at the magnificent architecture, the fabulous engineering feats, and the marvelous sculptures. You will learn about their living styles, transportation, science, literature, governments, and religions. And of course their wars—the conquests and defeats that caused the rise and fall of many great civilizations.

But first let's take a look at man's slow progress, step by step, which eventually led to the building and occupation of cities. Man had been on earth for more than two million years when true civilization began.*

*The term man is used in this book to mean the family of man, including women and children.

2

From the very beginning, manlike primates, not quite human, had something no other animal could claim—an inventive brain. These manlike creatures were animal-hunters and plant-gatherers. To kill an animal, they hit it with a club or a rock. But to skin the animal and cut up its meat, they needed tools. These they made by chipping off the edges of stones to make sharp cutting implements. This marked the beginning of the OLD STONE AGE.

As time went on, the early ancestors of today's humans evolved, generation after generation. Both their bodies and their brains improved, and so did the tools they made.

About ten thousand years ago, a new group of people appeared, and an era known as the NEOLITHIC AGE or NEW STONE AGE began. These Neolithic people had a more advanced culture than any that had existed previously, and their descendants later became the builders and inhabitants of the great cities and the developers of their culture.

Let's observe the early life and the progress of the Neolithic people.

THE NEOLITHIC AGE

10,000 to 4,000 Years Ago

About nine to ten thousand years ago, the Neolithic people appeared in Southwest Asia, North Africa, and the Balkan countries of Europe; that is, in the area we now call the Middle East. These people had been developing a more and more civilized way of life for many thousands of years. The details of their previous existence are not known, but it may be assumed that they led the lives of wanderers, following the wild animals and plants. They still lived the life of hunters and plant-gatherers, but they had many advanced tools and implements—axes and hammers of smoothly polished stone, sharp knives of flint, fishhooks and harpoons made of bone. And most important of all, these people invented the bow and arrow. A hunter no longer had to creep up close to kill an animal: it could be shot from a distance. They also domesticated the dog, which helped them hunt other animals.

The use of fire having been discovered much earlier, the Neolithic people apparently knew the art of cooking and preserving foods; this is evidenced by the clay pots and jars found in Neolithic deposits. These not only have been found in the Middle East, but recently have been discovered in places as far afield as Japan.

Over many generations, the Neolithic people discovered that they could plant wild seeds and cultivate them, thus beginning an early form of agriculture. They also learned to domesticate sheep and goats and, later, cattle and pigs.

By 5000 B.C., farmers were living in many parts of the world. Agricultural communities existed in what we now call western Greece, the Balkans, Hungary, Crete, and

Southeast Italy. Other groups of farmers made their way in crude ships to Sicily, Malta, North Africa, southern France, Spain, and Portugal. Britain was reached in about 3500 B.C.

A great advance for agriculture was the invention by farmers in Europe of an early form of the plow. At first this plow was drawn by humans, later by oxen.

After they had exhausted the soil of one plot of land, some farmers moved on to new areas. But now that they had their domestic livestock for food and milk, many chose to settle permanently in one place. In addition to growing fruits, grains, and vegetables, some raised flax, from which they could make thread and weave cloth for clothing, instead of wearing animal hides and skins.

About 6,500 years ago (4500 B.C.) farming was beginning to advance in Europe. However, by that time the Neolithic people in Southwest Asia had reached a more advanced stage. Some remained farmers, but others built huts and began to gather into villages. These people formed groups with an early form of government which was much stronger than the earlier rule of the wandering tribes. This became the nucleus of the first true civilization. Gradually the villages grew into towns and eventually into great cities—especially in the land called Mesopotamia.

NOTE: For more details and illustrations about early man, see the author's book *How Man Began.*

MESOPOTAMIA

SUMERIANS, BABYLONIANS, AND ASSYRIANS

3500 B.C. to 599 B.C.

By about 3500 B.C., several cities had arisen in western Asia, in Mesopotamia, a fertile strip of land between two great rivers, the Tigris and the Euphrates. One of the cities was called Sumer. Its inhabitants, the Sumerians, were an energetic and creative people.

The Sumerians were originally farmers and cattle breeders, but in time they produced an oversupply of farm products. Thus a new class of people arose, among them builders, craftsmen, priests, merchants, and traders. They spread throughout the land of Mesopotamia and developed a group of city-states. This was the earliest organized government, and it became the first center of civilized society.

6

The Sumerians became excellent metalworkers. At first they worked in copper, gold, and silver, all of which had been discovered previously. Then, in about 2500 B.C., they invented a method of adding a small amount of tin to copper, producing a new metal: BRONZE. Bronze was far stronger than any of the other metals known at the time. Its discovery marked the end of the NEOLITHIC AGE and the beginning of the BRONZE AGE.

The Bronze Age lasted about twelve hundred years and spread throughout the known world. Bronze armor and chariots were used in warfare. Although the wheel had been invented elsewhere, the Sumerians improved upon its design and were the first to attach wheels to carts and later to war chariots. The first pictures of wheeled carts pulled by oxen are shown on Sumerian clay tablets that date from about 3250 B.C.

There was no building stone available in Mesopotamia, but there was plenty of clay. The Sumerians made clay bricks and dried them in the sun. They built huge cities of bricks, among them Ur, Nineveh, and Babylon, mentioned in the Bible. Clay was also used for making pottery. At first the pottery was made by hand by rolling clay into strips and winding the strips around and around to form the shape of a jar or vase. But later the potter's wheel was introduced, making the shaping of pottery much easier. The Sumerians made many fine jars, vases, and various other vessels which they decorated with black designs.

The Sumerians were religious people, worshipping

many gods and goddesses. Each city had its temples devoted to certain deities. Among them were Anu, god of the heavens, Enlil, god of air, and Enki, god of water. If there was drought, flood, or disease, the priests carried out rituals to appease the gods. These often included human sacrifice.

Often, a building called a ziggurat stood beside a temple. This was a pyramidlike brick structure with several step terraces. It had a high tower with a room at the top for the use of the god when he came down to earth.

The Sumerians believed that their main purpose in life was to serve the gods, so they spent much of their time praying in the temples. They made stone statuettes of themselves with huge eyes and left them before the altars so that their prayers would continue even if they were not there in person.

The Sumerians invented a system of writing which they inscribed on clay tablets. The writing consisted of signs

Ziggurat

made up of V-shaped marks. It is called cuneiform writing after the Latin *cuneus,* meaning "wedge." It is also known as "nail-writing." These inscriptions were not deciphered until about two hundred years ago. It took many learned people about fifty years to work out a key to the symbols.

The Sumerians were expert mathematicians. They counted in tens, as we do today, and also in sixties. It was the Sumerians who divided the hour into sixty minutes and the minute into sixty seconds.

The Sumerians dominated Mesopotamia for more than a thousand years. In the meantime, some of the other strong city-states prospered, among them Babylon. Many of the individual rulers made war upon one another, trying to unite the country under a single government.

In about 2750 B.C., Sargon I, the king of Akkad (the northern portion of Mesopotamia, including Babylon), invaded and conquered Sumer, the southern part of the country. He united the two parts, creating the first great empire in history. He reigned for fifty-six years. After his death, however, the empire collapsed. But it was regained and lost a number of times during the next one thousand years.

After many wars between the city-states, the king of a desert tribe, King Hammurabi, took possession of the city of Babylon in 1792 B.C. Babylon had been a great city for about 300 years, but this great monarch made Babylon the leading power in Mesopotamia and surrounding lands.

Hammurabi reigned for forty-two years and waged many wars and made conquests during that time. He built himself a magnificent palace in Babylon, and, most importantly, he drew up for his people a set of laws which, judged by the standards of that time, were just and humane.

After Hammurabi's death, his kingdom fell into decay. The Hittites, a desert tribe who are thought to have been the first to make iron weapons, thus launching the IRON AGE, overran the valley. With their new iron weapons, they managed to destroy whatever they could not carry away. The Hittites invaded other areas as well and built a large empire. They were a dominant power in the Middle East for about three hundred years. However, their empire was destroyed in 1200 B.C. by the Assyrians, fierce warriors from an area north of Babylon who had learned the secrets of iron-working from the Hittites and improved on their weapons.

Over the next five hundred years, the Assyrians became a great power. Under the leadership of various kings, including Tiglath Pileser I, they made many conquests and developed a great civilization which rose and fell several times.

In about 720 B.C., a general usurped the Assyrian throne and named himself Sargon II after the early monarch, whom he greatly admired. Under his rule, the Assyrians conquered almost all of western Asia and gathered taxes from their many subjects.

Upon the death of Sargon II, in 705 B.C., his son Sennacherib continued the Assyrian conquests. He sacked and burned Babylon and made the five-hundred-year-old city of Nineveh the Assyrian capital. In 612 B.C., however, Nineveh, where some of the finest Assyrian sculptures have been found, was captured by the Chaldeans, another desert tribe. They reestablished Babylon as the capital and made it the most splendorous city in the world at that time. Their king, Nebuchadnezzar, ruled from 605 B.C. to 562 B.C. He encouraged the study of science. Much of our modern knowledge of astronomy and mathematics is based on certain principles which were first discovered by the Babylonians. They made star maps, observed the movements of the planets, and predicted eclipses of the sun and the moon.

The Babylonians were travelers and traders. Thousands of cuneiform tablets showing trading agreements and bills of lading have been found. They exported wool, woven fabrics, and barley. From Armenia they imported minerals, among other things.

Babylon fell to the Medes and the Persians in 539 B.C., during the reign of Belshazzar, the last of the Babylonian kings. Two centuries later it was conquered again, this time by Alexander the Great, who planned to revive the city. But four years later his early death at the age of thirty-two caused his kingdom to become divided, and Babylon fell into decay. All that remains today are a few ruins.

HEBREWS AND PHOENICIANS

3000 B.C. to A.D. 135

Mesopotamia is sometimes called the Land of the Bible. The Hebrews had lived in Mesopotamia and eastern Syria from about 3000 B.C., in the area known in the Old Testament as Canaan. (Syria is not to be confused with *Assyria,* the homeland of the ancient Assyrians.) In about 2000 B.C., Abraham left his home in the city of Ur in Sumer, reaching Canaan in about 1950 B.C. The Hebrews lived in this land, which was later called Palestine and now is known as Israel, until about 1600 B.C., when a great famine ravaged the land. This drove the Hebrews to migrate into Egypt. There they lived until 1200 B.C., when a young leader named Moses helped them return to Canaan.

The Hebrews made astonishing contributions to literature, history, and poetry, much of it contained in the Old Testament.

Another Mesopotamian people, the Phoenicians, lived at about the same time. They occupied the narrow strip of land known today as Lebanon. Originally farmers, they later became craftsmen, merchants, and, most importantly, shipbuilders and seagoing traders. They made textiles of wool and flax, and jewelry of ivory, gold, and gems. They extracted a purple dye from a kind of shellfish, and this was used to color the royal robes. They made long journeys by sea, trading their manufactured goods and artistic works for grain, livestock, and timber to build their ships. They also imported metals, including tin and iron. The seamen established trading posts in many different countries.

One of the most important contributions of the Phoenicians to modern-day culture was the alphabet which we use today. The cuneiform writing of Mesopotamia and the picture writing of the Egyptians were common all over western Asia, but it was the Phoenicians who invented the modern alphabet, in which each character stands for a sound rather than for a word or an idea. Inscriptions in alphabetic writing date back to 1300 B.C.

EGYPT

THE OLD KINGDOM

3200 B.C. to 2050 B.C.

Egypt's civilization apparently began about three hundred years later than Mesopotamia's, but it lasted six hundred years longer. Unlike the early Sumerians, whose civilization consisted of city-states without a central government, the Egyptians became the first ancient people to achieve nationhood. A series of kings called pharaohs ruled the Egyptians for a period of thirty-five hundred years. The Egyptians considered the pharaohs gods as well as rulers.

The most important factor in the settlement of Egypt was the River Nile. This river flows from south to north six hundred miles through the full length of the country. Although almost all of Egypt was desert land, as it is even today, the Nile overflowed every summer, leaving a coat

14

of mud over the valley. The first Egyptians, who were wandering hunters and herdsmen, learned to sow seeds in this mud, and they found that it produced grain. The women probably planted while the men hunted with the dogs they had domesticated, but it is likely that the whole family took part in the reaping and other such chores. These early Egyptians also bred sheep, goats, and cattle. They learned to weave cloth of the flax which they planted. They also made pottery jars by hand and used them for preserving their food.

The flooding of the Nile was not dependable, however. Sometimes it would overflow too much and cause destructive floods. Another time, it might not flood enough, and there would be famine. Gradually the farmers began to band together, building dikes to control the water. They also stored grain for their use in the years when their crops failed.

The benefits of the Nile were not confined to the valley. The Egyptians built a system of canals and irrigation trenches that carried water all over the land.

By about 3400 B.C., there were two separate kingdoms in Egypt. The region around the Nile delta was called Lower Egypt, and the rest was called Upper Egypt. They existed together for about two hundred years. Then in 3200 B.C., a king called Menes conquered the northern part and became the first King of Upper and Lower Egypt. From that time on, Egyptian history was divided into three parts—the Old Kingdom, the Middle Kingdom, and the New Kingdom.

The Old Kingdom lasted from 2800 B.C. to 2050 B.C., during which time the famous pyramids at Giza were built. The Egyptians had a strong belief that life went on after death. When a person died, the relatives had his body embalmed, wrapped in yards of linen and put into a coffin, then buried in a tomb or grave. To make the dead person comfortable on his journey to the underworld, the grave was filled with things he might need. There were furniture, musical instruments, food, jewels, and sometimes many little statues of servants, cooks, and bakers. Very often, robbers broke into these graves and stole the jewels and other contents. To prevent this, mounds of stones were built on top of the graves. The rich people built higher and higher mounds which eventually became colossal burial monuments, the pyramids of the kings. The largest of these was built by King Cheops, who reigned from 2650 B.C. to 2630 B.C. Sometimes called the Great Pyramid, it is 450 feet high, covers more than thirteen acres, and contains nearly six million tons of stone. The king's body was placed in a granite chamber at its center.

Alongside the Cheops pyramid are two somewhat smaller pyramids ordered by his son and grandson, who succeeded him as kings. Guarding the three pyramids is the Sphinx, a giant statue representing the king with the body of a lion, showing the strength and power of the rulers.

These pyramids are still in existence today, at least forty-five hundred years after they were built. Perhaps the most baffling aspect of their architecture is that their builders had no iron tools or wheeled vehicles. They had to haul huge stone blocks, each weighing as much as fifteen tons, from the quarries many miles away. It is believed that they may have carried the stones on ferryboats across the Nile, then hauled them to the construction site on sledges and pulled them up ramps of mud with ropes made from the papyrus plant. It took as many as a hundred thousand men about twenty years to build one pyramid.

Education enjoyed a high place in Ancient Egypt. The Egyptians invented a method of writing with picture signs. This was entirely different from the cuneiform writing of Mesopotamia. The Egyptian system of writing

The Great Pyramid and Sphinx

17

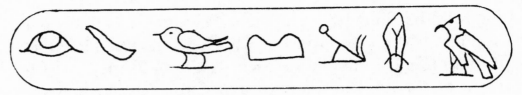

Hieroglyphics

is called hieroglyphics, from the Greek for sacred writing. They wrote their history on joined strips of material made from the papyrus plant. The writing was not deciphered until the year 1799 of our present era, when a French officer serving in the Nile delta looked around at the ruins and found a stone covered with figures. It carried three inscriptions—one of them in Greek. By comparing the Greek words with the hieroglyphics, a French professor deciphered some of the symbols. Over a period of twenty years of study, the Egyptian writing became understandable. From many Egyptian papyrus manuscripts and the excavations of archeologists, the history of the valley of the Nile has been rediscovered.

The priests and scribes, who could read and write, were held in high esteem in Egypt. In order to read hieroglyphics, it was necessary to memorize about seven hundred separate signs. The Egyptians also evolved a system of mathematics to use in their business dealings and their architecture. They named and mapped the stars, and they recorded a body of literature.

Egyptian doctors and surgeons were famous throughout the ancient world. They studied human anatomy while preparing bodies for embalming, and they experimented with the healing properties of various plants and other substances. Although they were still using superstitious practices, some of the treatments they recommended for illness have been approved by modern medical doctors.

Many of the less educated people were excellent craftsmen who learned to work copper and stone, to weave baskets, and to make pottery with the potter's wheel, which may have been brought from western Asia. They made sculptures and paintings and decorated their pottery with beautiful designs.

THE MIDDLE KINGDOM

2050 B.C. to 1580 B.C.

During the Middle Kingdom, Egypt was attacked by foreign armies. The Hyksos, a desert tribe from Syria and Palestine, finally defeated the Egyptians and ruled from 1700 B.C. to 1580 B.C. Then Ahmose, a prince from Thebes, a city on the Nile, drove the Hyksos out and launched the New Kingdom at Thebes. This began a glorious new empire beyond the dreams of the earlier Egyptians.

THE NEW KINGDOM

1580 B.C. to 1085 B.C.

From the Hyksos the Egyptians had acquired new and more reliable iron weapons and the light horse-drawn chariot. The pharaohs and their armies embarked on conquest of the great powers of western Asia. The soldiers, now helmeted and dressed in coats of mail, stormed into battle, led by the king in his gilded chariot. The armies had many successes and they returned to Egypt with great treasures, as well as prisoners, who became slaves.

During the New Kingdom the kings were no longer buried in pyramids; their tombs were sunk deep into the rock. There, it was believed, they would be safe from grave robbers. Nevertheless, the graves were robbed. It was by a stroke of good luck that one of the greatest finds in the history of archeology was discovered intact as recently as the year 1922. It was the tomb of the boy-king Tutankhamen, who died in the year 1352 B.C. at the early age of nineteen. The tomb was loaded with jewels, ornaments, and other furnishings—all representing the finest craftsmanship of Egypt's imperial age. A mask of solid gold covered the head of the mummy of Tutankhamen, representing him as Osiris, the god of the underworld.

The glories of the New Kingdom lasted about six hundred years, a short time compared to the three-thousand-year history of Egypt, but still three times as long as the history of the United States of America up to the present.

THE LATER PERIOD

1085 B.C. to A.D. 300

In the year 1085 B.C., following the death of King Ramses II, corruption in the government brought on civil uprisings. This, together with new attempts by foreign invaders to capture Egypt, brought a decline in the arts and culture, which had reached a pinnacle at that time.

When Assyria conquered all of western Asia in the eighth century B.C., Egypt became a part of the Assyrian Empire. But within a hundred years, Egypt once more became an independent state under a new line of kings. Prosperity returned, the arts were revived, trade flourished, and friendship with Greece was fostered.

In 525 B.C. Egypt was conquered by Cambyses, the king of Persia, who made it into a province of the great Persian Empire. Two centuries later, Alexander the Great of Macedonia (a Greek province), who had conquered most of the known world, entered Egypt and forced the last of

21

the Persian governors to surrender. Upon Alexander's death in 323 B.C., his empire was divided among his generals. One of them set himself up as king of a new Egyptian state in the city of Alexandria, which Alexander had recently built. The new pharaoh called himself Ptolemy I and was the first king in the dynasty of the Ptolemies.

During the reign of Ptolemy I (323 B.C. to 285 B.C.), the city of Alexandria came to be known throughout the world as a great center of learning. Ptolemy set up the Alexandria Museum, which was actually the first university in history. It was mostly devoted to the study of science and Greek philosophy. Renowned professors and students came to Alexandria from many parts of the world. The medical school enjoyed great fame, and doctors came there to study the advances in medical science.

It was at the Alexandria Museum that the great Greek mathematician Euclid developed a system of geometry, the basis of today's method of computing the measurements of planes and solids. There also the Greek astronomer Aristarchus decided that the sun, not the earth, was the center of the universe.

Side by side with the Museum, Ptolemy created the great Library of Alexandria. Hundreds of scrolls recording the history of Egypt and manuscripts brought from many places in the world were catalogued and stored there. This provided the greatest source of recorded knowledge of the time.

Ptolemy I was succeeded by Ptolemy II, who ruled

from 285 B.C. to about 247 B.C. Egypt continued to prosper and its culture flourished.

During this time, wealthy Egyptians enjoyed a gracious life. They lived in comfortable villas, ate good food, had well-stocked wine cellars, and concerned themselves with music and the other arts.

After the death of Ptolemy II, the rulers became less powerful, for the priests of the old religions dominated them. The support of the arts and sciences regressed, and the Alexandria Museum remained in existence only about a hundred years before its influence died out. As time went on, the power of Egypt diminished.

In the meantime, the Romans had set out to conquer the world. In 39 B.C. they arrived in Egypt. Queen Cleopatra tried to save her country by forming an alliance with the great Roman leader Julius Caesar, and later with Mark Antony. But her romantic efforts did not rescue Egypt from the Roman invaders. Later, Cleopatra tried to win the affections of Octavian, Caesar's successor as the military and naval leader of Rome, but she did not succeed. Cleopatra, greatly disappointed, killed herself and thus ended the Egyptian dynasties.

Egypt continued its existence under Roman rule. But the introduction of Christianity caused the old Egyptian religions to die out. The temples fell into decay; the tombs and their occupants were forgotten. After thirty-five hundred years, the civilization of the Nile passed into history in about A.D. 300.

GREECE

THE MINOANS

3000 B.C. to 1400 B.C.

Up to about a hundred years ago, historians believed that Greek civilization began around the year 800 B.C. However, in the past century, archeological excavations made in the Aegean Islands off the coast of Greece show that civilizations were flourishing there as long ago as 3000 B.C. In A.D. 1900, Sir Arthur Evans, an English archeologist, uncovered ruins of the buried city of Knossos on the island of Crete.

Evans found the remains of a tremendous palace, covering six acres of ground. The palace, which was apparently the home of the king and queen, consisted of many connected rooms. There were great banquet halls and workshops, a religious center, and large cellars with

24

storerooms for oil, wine, and grain. The brilliantly colored paintings which covered many of the walls were done with a high level of artistic skill, and many retain their lovely colors even now, five thousand years later.

Many surprisingly modern features were found in this palace. There were stoves, bathrooms, and excellent drainage systems.

The city of Knossos may have had as many as a hundred thousand inhabitants—a tremendous population for that time. These people were called the Minoans, after their king, Minos. From relics found, it has been determined that the Minoans were seagoing traders. They apparently sailed in primitive boats to the coasts of Spain, Egypt, and North Africa. They traded their wine, olive oil, beautiful jewelry and art objects for tin, gold, ivory, and pearls, among other things.

Clay tablets found in the ruins show that these people had a form of writing which today is called Linear A. It is the first script in which the letters are arranged in horizontal lines. Unfortunately, this early script has not been deciphered as yet.

Apparently, the Minoans lived in peace and prosperity for more than a thousand years. But in about 1400 B.C., the Minoan civilization disappeared. No one knows exactly what happened. It is suggested that there may have been a violent earthquake which buried the city of Knossos as well as many other cities nearby. (The Aegean Islands are subject to earthquakes even today.) Or the city may have been invaded by barbaric tribes who demolished everything.

THE MYCENAEANS

1900 B.C. to 1100 B.C.

Five hundred years before the disappearance of the Minoans, mainland Greece was occupied by illiterate farmers and sheepherders still using stone tools and living a primitive life in crude huts. It is believed that in about 1900 B.C. a fierce warrior tribe came down from the north and attacked the inhabitants. These warriors had weapons and tools of bronze, in contrast to the stone tools of the farmers. The warriors easily overcame the stone-agers. They conquered the area on the mainland of Greece called Mycenae.

These conquerors were tall, strong, bearded men. They were rough, illiterate, and full of fight. They worshipped Zeus, a god of storms and violence. Over a period of time, they also attacked the people on the islands off the coast of Greece, including the Minoans, and they learned to imitate Minoan arts and crafts.

In time these people, who are now known as the Mycenaeans, became very wealthy. The warlords lived in great splendor in fabulous castles surrounded by thick stone walls.

In 1194 B.C., the Mycenaeans declared war on Troy, a city in Asia Minor, on the opposite shore of the Aegean Sea. The reason for the war was supposedly that a Trojan prince, Paris, had stolen the love of Helen, the wife of the Mycenaean king, Menelaus. Paris had kidnapped Helen and taken her to Troy. The Mycenaeans fought many bloody battles with the Trojans, and at last, after ten years, they defeated Troy and rescued Helen.

Stories of the brave Greek heroes were told by their people and handed down from generation to generation. One of the favorite legends was the story of the Trojan War. But since there was no written language in Greece at that time, the tales were not recorded until about 400 years later, after the Greeks had become literate. They borrowed the Phoenician alphabet and improved upon it. The Phoenicians used only consonants in their alphabet, but the Greeks added vowels, which made it possible to represent the sounds of a word more definitely.

By 800 B.C., the Greeks had a beautiful written language. At this time Homer, possibly the greatest poet in history, wrote a long story-poem about the Trojan War.

Greek inscription

He called it the *Iliad,* from Ilium, the Greek name for Troy, and it became a classic that is honored to this day. Until little more than a hundred years ago, scholars thought that the tale was purely a myth and insisted that Troy had never existed. But a German named Heinrich Schliemann did believe the story. He read the *Iliad* over and over again, and decided that he would go to look for the city of Troy.

In the 1870s, Schliemann headed for the exact area in Hissarlik, Turkey, where Homer had placed the city of Troy in the *Iliad.* In spite of the fact that the story of Troy was considered mythical, Schliemann was convinced that the city had existed. Over a period of several years, at his own expense and under great hardships, Schliemann carried on excavations. Finally he uncovered four different cities built one on top of the other. The second from the top was indeed Troy! Here were the great Trojan Wall and the Trojan Tower as described in the *Iliad,* as well as many artifacts related to the period. The Trojan War became a historical reality.

Schliemann found a city at least a thousand years older,

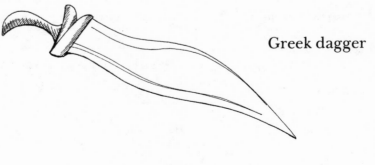

Greek dagger

Death mask of Agamemnon

buried beneath Troy. Here he discovered many beautiful
art works, statuettes, items of jewelry, and decorated
vases. He was convinced that these were examples of
Mycenaean art. So he proceeded to the ancient site of
Mycenae, where he found many rich treasures. In the
royal tombs, which scholars had said did not exist, there
were solid gold death masks of kings, glorious gold
crowns for queens, and superb bowls, daggers, and wine
cups. This proved that the Mycenaeans were wealthy and
powerful people of their time, and that they undoubtedly
were the people who fought Troy.

THE DORIAN GREEKS

After 1100 B.C.

In about 1100 B.C., hordes of invaders from the Balkan areas poured into mainland Greece. They were called the Dorians. They were crude, uneducated barbarians who spoke a Greek dialect. They carried spears and daggers made of iron—a new development in weapons in this part of the world. With these the Dorians were able to defeat many of the Mycenaean inhabitants, who had only bronze weapons. Some groups, however, were able to resist the invaders and retain their own way of life. They proudly told stories of their brave Mycenaean ancestors, and each generation continued to hand down the tales to their descendants.

At first, the Dorians settled in small villages. But gradually the villages grew into cities, each a small city-state in its own right. The cities remained independent rather than trying to unite with each other. The two most important city-states were Athens and Sparta. Neither of them had more than 20,000 inhabitants. The two cities were quite different from each other. The Athenians

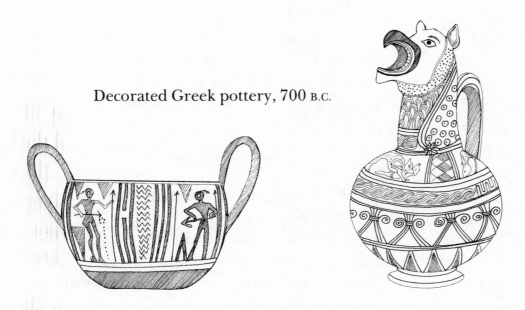

Decorated Greek pottery, 700 B.C.

loved knowledge and the arts. They tried to live a peaceful life, developing literature, the theater, architecture, sports, and sculpture, and worshipping their many gods. Sparta, on the other hand, was purely a military-minded city. At the age of seven, boys were put into camps and trained to take harsh treatment. This produced the finest soldiers in Greece, but very little culture. Sometimes when Athens was engaged in wars, Sparta came to her aid, but as time went on, the two city-states became implacable enemies, and finally went to war against each other.

Beginning in about 750 B.C., and for the next century or more, the inhabitants of mainland Greece sailed out and founded colonies on the islands off the coast of Greece. They also settled in southern Italy, Sicily, and the west coast of Asia Minor, called Ionia. By 700 B.C., the Greeks were trading with more than one hundred cities in the Greek colonies. They sold oil, wine, jewelry, pottery, and sculpture, and they bought such things as cereals and metals.

The Greeks believed in the beauty of simplicity in all things. Their houses, made of mud bricks which had been dried in the sun, were mostly cube-shaped and, like the Greek statues, were painted in bright colors. Athens, as well as some other important Greek cities, was built on high ground, which could be easily defended in time of war. The central hill of Athens was called the Acropolis.

The Greeks worshipped many gods and goddesses, who had human faults as well as virtues. Zeus, who supposedly lived on Mount Olympus, was believed to be the king of gods and men. His anger was expressed in thunder, lightning, and storms. He was said to compete with earthly men for their wives, and he would carry a human female off to his mountain home when he chose. This angered Hera, his wife, who would take revenge, usually on the woman rather than on Zeus himself. Poseidon, the brother of Zeus, was the god of the sea. He lived deep down in the ocean and was thought to cause sea storms and earthquakes. The underworld was ruled by Pluto and Persephone, who lived in Hades. These are just a few of the many gods to whom the Greeks built temples, which they filled with beautiful statues. Some of the others were Athena, goddess of wisdom; Apollo, god of the sun; Artemis, goddess of the moon and hunting; Aphrodite, goddess of love and beauty; Ares, god of war; Hermes, messenger of the gods; Hestia, goddess of the hearth; Eros, god of love.

Over a period of two to three hundred years, some Greeks became great artists. They produced beautiful buildings, statues, painted vases and jars. The sculptors were especially talented in portraying the human body. A healthy, well-built body was admired by men and women alike. To develop their bodies, Greek youths competed in many forms of sports.

In about 776 B.C., a great religious festival honoring Zeus was held in the city of Olympia. The most important feature of this event was the running contests. Athletes from all parts of Greece and the colonies came to Olympia to compete with each other. This was the beginning of the Olympic Games, which took place every four years.

Later, other competitions were added—boxing, jumping, javelin and discus throwing, wrestling, and chariot races. The games continued over a period of about six hundred years, but were discontinued by order of the Romans after they had conquered Greece in 146 B.C. The Olympic Games of modern times were revived in Athens in A.D. 1896 and are still held every four years in various places in the world.

Politics in Athens

At first, the Dorians had been simple, hard-working peasants. But as time went on, certain people among them became greedy and started to fight with the others. The winners of the fights wound up with an unfair share of the farms and estates. They formed a class of wealthy nobles who ruled over the working classes. These aristocratic nobles were continually quarreling among themselves to decide which one should rule over all the others. The one who emerged victorious became a sort of king who was called a Tyrant. The word "tyrant" did not have the same meaning then that it has today. Some Tyrants were good, some fair, and some very bad.

At this time, there were no set laws governing the people of Athens. A Tyrant named Draco was called upon to draw up a body of laws to govern the people and to protect them from injustices the nobles might impose upon them. Draco set up a code of laws, but they were so harsh it was almost impossible to enforce them. To Draco, a crime was a crime, and there was no such thing as compassion or leniency in dealing with an offender. A person might be sentenced to death for such a minor offense as stealing a handful of raisins.

About thirty years later, Solon, a kinder Tyrant who was also a great statesman, laid out a set of more balanced laws. His laws gave each citizen a voice in running the government. This was the beginning of the first democratic government in the world.

There were three classes of people in Athens: the wealthy nobles, the free citizens who either had been born in Athens or were the sons of Athenians, and the slaves. The slaves and women were not allowed to vote. The judges of the law courts were elected from the class of nobles. To protect the poorer classes, who ran the risk of being judged unfairly by the nobles, Solon provided that a citizen be given the right to state his case before a jury of thirty of his fellow Athenians.

Solon's laws also provided that each citizen of Athens had a responsibility for the safety and prosperity of the city-state. A citizen's first duty, before everything else, was to attend all meetings of the town council and become aware of what was happening in government.

In this free atmosphere, Athens could no longer tolerate Tyrants, and so dispensed with them. Now the cultural growth of Greece was given a chance to blossom.

THE THREAT FROM THE PERSIANS

In the meantime Persia, which lay on the ancient trade routes between Asia and Europe, was developing a civilization of its own. Persia was one of the oldest countries in

Asia. Its first settlers, who came from Central Asia, began to live near the Persian Gulf in about 6000 B.C., at least three thousand years before the earliest Greeks. These early settlers practiced a simple form of agriculture and were fine potters and goldsmiths. As time went on, some of them became merchants who brought silks, spices, gold, and perfumes to the west, trading for other goods.

In about 1000 B.C. there was a great rush of people into Persia from the Caucasus Mountain areas. At first, they established two separate countries—the Kingdom of the Medes (south of the Caspian Sea) and the Kingdom of Persia (east of the Persian Gulf). For several centuries these two rival kingdoms existed independently. But finally, in the sixth century B.C., an ambitious monarch, Cyrus the Great, came into power in Persia. He attacked the Medes, conquered them, and united the two kingdoms, at least doubling his territory. His victory encouraged him, and he set about to establish a great empire.

Cyrus invaded and conquered Assyria, Babylonia, the steppes of Central Asia, and lands as far east as India. Among his principal conquests were the Greek colonies on the coastlands of Asia Minor, and he hoped to invade mainland Greece as well. In 546 B.C., he united all his conquests into one empire—the greatest empire on earth up to that time.

Greece continued to prosper for another half century after Cyrus conquered the Greek colonies in Asia Minor, but the threat of this powerful new empire hung over them.

Cyrus died in 529 B.C. and was succeeded by his son, Cambyses II, who continued his father's building of the Persian Empire. In 525 B.C. he conquered Egypt and made it a Persian province. Upon his death in 521 B.C. he was succeeded by his cousin, Darius I, who called himself the "King of Kings." He divided the empire into twenty provinces and required each to pay heavy taxes to Persia.

The Greeks in Asia Minor were greatly dissatisfied with the rule of Darius and the burden of taxes they had to pay, and they revolted against Persia. Darius considered the rebellious Greeks politically dangerous, because they provided a bad example to all other Persian subjects who were forced to be obedient to the emperor. He therefore gathered his troops, invaded the coastland city-states, and crushed the revolt. Then, having decided to capture all of Greece by invading Athens, he called on the Phoenicians for aid.

The Phoenicians, who were angry with Greece for trading in the Mediterranean, sent Darius a fleet of ships to help him attack Greece. The ships carrying the Persian soldiers sailed across the Aegean Sea and landed in the bay near the village of Marathon, a short way from Athens. As soon as the Athenians heard of the arrival of the Persians, they sent an army of ten thousand men to guard Marathon, and they dispatched Pheidippides, their fastest runner, to Sparta for help. But Sparta, always jealous of Athens, refused to send aid. So did all the other Greek cities except the tiny town of Plataea, which sent a thousand men.

On September 12, 490 B.C., the Athenian commander Miltiades led his small spear-bearing army against the poorly organized Persian multitude, who fought with arrows. The Greeks had devised a military formation called a phalanx, in which the men interlocked shields to form a solid wall of armor. Thus they won a tremendous victory, and that night they set fire to the Persian ships. As they watched the sky grow red with flames, the people of Athens wondered whether they were winning or losing. Finally a runner appeared. It was Pheidippides, who had

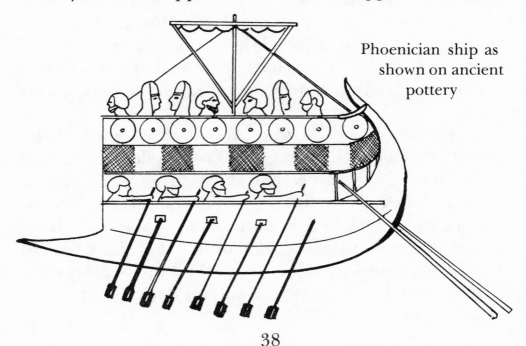

Phoenician ship as
shown on ancient
pottery

returned to Marathon from his run to Sparta and had then volunteered to bring the news of the Greek victory to Athens, a distance of 26 miles, 385 yards. He whispered, "We have won," and then fell dead. (Today's Marathon races, patterned after the run from Marathon to Athens, are exactly as long as the distance run by Pheidippides.) After their defeat by the Greeks at Marathon, the Persians disappeared and Greece was again at peace, though not for long.

Nine years later, in 481 B.C., King Xerxes, the successor to Darius, assembled the hugest army the world had ever seen, and built a large navy, which consisted mostly of Phoenician ships and sailors. This great force moved against a province in northern Greece. This time Sparta,

Greek runners

realizing the danger to itself, led the defense on land, while Athens, with a small but well-equipped navy, was prepared to battle the Persian fleet at sea.

The Spartan commander, Leonidas, with only a small group of soldiers, guarded the narrow road between the mountains and the sea connecting Thessaly with the southern provinces. He held the pass valiantly, but Ephialtes, a Greek traitor, took a regiment of Persians through the hills, which he knew well, and the Persians were able to attack Leonidas from the rear. A terrible battle was fought near Thermopylae. Leonidas and his soldiers were killed, as were almost all the Persians.

The loss of the mountain pass allowed the Persians to conquer the greater part of Greece. They marched into Athens and burned the city, and the people of Athens had to flee. Athenian ships carried many of the citizens to safety on the island of Salamis. Then they attacked the Persian fleet within the narrow straits between Salamis and the mainland, destroying three-fourths of the Persian ships. King Xerxes took his troops back to Thessaly and waited until spring to try again for a victory over the Greeks.

But by spring a dozen different Greek cities, including Sparta, had formed a united army of a hundred thousand men. They attacked the Persian army, which had three times as many men, near Plataea, and defeated them completely. This time, the Persians left, never to return.

Athens Rebuilds

Just after the Persian wars, in the 5th century B.C., a great leader named Pericles arose in Athens. He was an aristocrat with a dream of restoring even more beauty and glory to the city than it had ever had before. He was also a democrat who believed in the rights of all Greek citizens.

During Pericles' time, Athens instituted an association of more than two hundred city-states which was called the Delian League. They were not unified into a single state but were allied to help protect the Athenian possessions from the Persian kings. This defensive alliance helped give Athens a period of peace lasting about fifty years— and a period of culture without parallel in history.

Under Pericles, almost the complete city of Athens was rebuilt. On the Acropolis, which had become a religious center, he built a breathtakingly magnificent marble temple to the goddess Athena, after whom Athens had been named. This temple was called the Parthenon. Its beautiful design, with row after row of pillars, represents the height of Greek art and taste, and has influenced architecture throughout the Western world to the present day. In front of the temple, Phidias, one of the greatest of all sculptors, created a forty-foot statue of Athena in ivory and gold.

The Parthenon

Pericles attracted the greatest creative minds and artists to Athens. The most talented architects, the most admired sculptors, and the finest craftsmen all flocked to the great cultural center. Some of the most famous plays of all time were written during this period. Aeschylus, who fought in the Greco-Persian War, wrote *The Persians*, the oldest surviving Greek play. Sophocles and Euripides, his two equally famous successors, wrote tragic dramas. The plays were produced and performed in vast open-air theaters seating as many as 14,000 spectators. They set a pattern for drama which is often the basis of plays today.

During this time, several of the world's greatest philosophers, men searching for the meaning of life, lived in Athens. The most famous of these was Socrates, who walked around Athens making speeches to anyone who would listen. In this way he spread his ideas and beliefs. He taught, among many other things, that a person

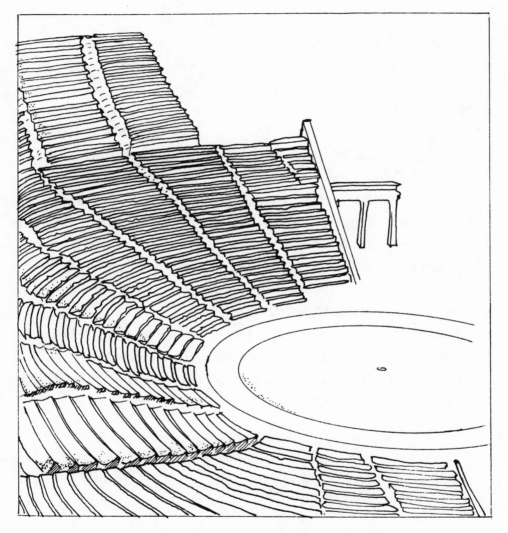

Greek amphitheater where plays were performed

should act according to reason and should not allow the mind to be guided by myths and superstitions. These teachings were interpreted by some people to mean that Socrates did not believe in the gods. At age seventy, he was brought to trial, charged with disloyalty to the gods and with corrupting the minds of the youth. He was sentenced to death by drinking poison hemlock. He might have been pardoned had he changed his views. But this he would not do. He drank the hemlock and died bravely.

One of Socrates' most brilliant pupils was Plato. He wrote many essays explaining the philosophy of Socrates, and he also wrote down his own ideas. He believed that the greatest virtues were justice, courage, and wisdom. He founded a great educational institution called the Academy. He taught there for the rest of his life, and the school lived after him for 900 years.

Plato's most famous pupil was Aristotle. He propounded the concept of "moderation in all things." The practical use of this idea may be observed in Greek architecture, art, and life style.

SPARTA AND ATHENS AT WAR

Over a period of about three hundred years, there were many quarrels between Athens and Sparta. Finally, in 431 B.C., war was declared between the two old city-states. Shortly after the war began, a devastating plague broke out in Athens, and one-fourth to one-half of the Athenians lost their lives, among them the great leader Pericles, who died in 429 B.C.

In spite of the saddened spirit and great personal grief of the Athenians, the soldiers continued to fight, and the brilliant culture of Athens continued in spite of the war.

The war between Athens and Sparta lasted for twenty-seven years. Finally, in 404 B.C., Sparta, which had been building its military power for many years, forced Athens to make peace. The Spartan victory destroyed the dominance of Athens forever.

The defeated Athens, ruled by Spartans, tempted other powerful leaders to move in. King Philip of Macedonia, a great military state north of Greece, defeated the Spartan rulers of Athens in about 345 B.C. He united most of the Greek city-states and made himself the master of all Greece. Then he planned an attack on the Persians to repay them for their invasion of Greece a hundred and fifty years before. Before he could get started on this expedition, however, Philip was murdered by one of his bodyguards. It is believed his assassination, which took place at the wedding of his daughter, was plotted by Greeks who resented his takeover of their country.

ALEXANDER THE GREAT

King Philip's son, Alexander, took up where his father had left off. He was determined to build a world empire under the rule of Greece.

In 334 B.C., shortly after the death of his father, the twenty-two-year-old Alexander set forth with 35,000 troops to conquer the world. He invaded Asia Minor and freed the Greek cities there from Persian rule. Then he occupied Syria and Phoenicia and went on to invade Egypt, where he was proclaimed pharaoh. He founded his own city, Alexandria, which became the greatest port in the Mediterranean and the center of Greek science, literature, and arts. He defeated the last Persian king, Darius III, then continued as far east as India, overthrowing the entire Persian empire and bringing their territories under Greek rule, all in the short period of eight years.

After reaching India, Alexander's troops refused to go farther, as they believed that when they reached the ocean they would fall off the end of the earth. Alexander was forced to turn back, so he built a fleet and divided his forces, taking the main army back along the coast to the Persian Gulf. The soldiers suffered terribly, and many

Greek warrior

men died of thirst. The fleet followed him on the sea, meeting him at the Persian Gulf. The trip back took two years. On the way, Alexander fought many battles with strange peoples and founded many cities. He insisted that all the people be taught the Greek language, and that all cities be built in the Greek style of architecture, just as had been done in all his previous conquests.

In 323 B.C., Alexander reached Babylon, and there he occupied the old palace of King Hammurabi. Although he was filled with the glory of his conquests, he succumbed to a fever and soon died at the age of thirty-two.

Alexander had made no plans for a successor to his empire, so there was a great struggle for power among his most important generals. First they cleared the way by murdering Alexander's wife Roxanne and the son she had borne, also named Alexander. Then the three leading generals divided the empire among themselves. Ptolemy got Egypt and became the first of a long line of pharaohs bearing this name. He made Alexandria his principal city. He also kept Cyprus and most of the coast of Phoenicia and Asia Minor under his control. A general named Seleucus received much of the old Persian empire and founded the Seleucid dynasty. Antigonus got a large part of Asia Minor and founded a separate dynasty.

These three rulers and their successors carried on a civilization made up of Greek, Persian, Egyptian, and Babylonian elements for about two centuries after the death of Alexander. However, for several centuries,

Decorated Greek vase, 480 B.C.

Rome had been developing her culture and expanding her possessions. In the course of time, the Roman legions conquered Sicily, Sardinia, Corsica, southern Spain, parts of Asia Minor, and Alexander's own homeland, Macedonia. At last, in 146 B.C., the Romans invaded and conquered the Greek mainland, making Greece a Roman protectorate.

The cultural influences of Alexander's empire and the arts, architecture, literature, and crafts of the Greeks were made a part of their world by the Romans. Although the Greek motherland died, the glory that was Greece lived on and was spread throughout the western world by the Romans.

ROME

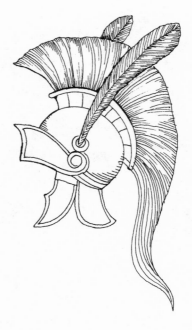

THE BEGINNINGS

1000 B.C. to 509 B.C.

Rome was founded in about 753 B.C., but people apparently had lived there prior to that time. Recent archeological excavations in the area have produced human bones dating back to 950 B.C., by which date, presumably, people had moved into Italy from Central Europe.

The earliest settlers were farmers and sheepherders. There were about a dozen different tribes, and they spoke an early form of Latin. They formed villages on seven small hills to the east and south of the Tiber River, and they called the land where they settled Latium. On the rocky top of the highest hill, the Capitoline Hill, they built religious shrines for worshipping their many gods. The shrines were surrounded by fortifications so that people could take refuge there in time of danger.

Just across the river from Latium was a land called Etruria. The origin of its people, called Etruscans, is debatable. Some scholars believe they came to Italy from Asia Minor, whereas others think they had lived in Italy for thousands of years. In any event, by the time the Latins arrived, the Etruscans were enjoying an advanced civilization. They had grown wealthy from trade and industry. They had established cities where only villages of huts had existed before. They had many ships and they shared power over the western end of the Mediterranean Sea with Carthage, the great seaport and trading center established by the Phoenicians about a thousand years earlier.

The Latins realized that they could learn a great deal from contact with the Etruscans. To make their association easier, they built a bridge across a narrow part of the Tiber River to connect Latium with Etruria. On an island in the middle of the river, they established a center where people could come to buy and sell merchandise. This was the beginning of Roman enterprise and became the foundation of the city of Rome itself.

The Etruscans, in their far-flung ventures, apparently traded with some of the colonies which Greece had established in the South of Italy. From Greek colonists, the Etruscans learned many of their arts: painting, ceramics, sculpture in clay and bronze, and jewelry making. In addition to their acquired arts and crafts, the Etruscans had a well-developed knowledge of engineering. They had an advanced form of architecture, including the arch, which was not only beautiful but was also an important step forward in structural design. The Etruscans passed on their artistic skill to the Romans, also teaching them how to plan towns and to build roads, bridges, drainage systems, and aqueducts. And they imparted to the Romans their knowledge of medicine, cooking, and astronomy.

The Romans adopted the architecture of the Etruscan temples, as well as many of their religious practices. The Etruscans, in spite of their comparatively advanced civilization, indulged in barbaric practices led by superstitious priests. The priests claimed they could foretell the success of any future event by cutting open a chicken or other animal and examining the quivering liver while the creature was still alive and bleeding. From this, they attempted to predict whether the time was right for beginning any venture. If the priests' prediction was unfavorable, the project was postponed, even if it was to be the launching of a war.

As time went on, this ritual was adopted by the Romans and became a part of their religious practices, eventually leading to the cruel sacrifice of human beings.

The Romans gave the title of *Pontifex Maximus,* meaning "chief bridge-builder," to their high priest. (The Pope, who is the bishop of Rome, is still called the Pontiff.)

Another custom of the Etruscans was the funeral games, of which gladiatorial fights were the leading feature. Male slaves or prisoners were pitted against each other, armed with swords or other weapons. They were

52

forced to fight until one or the other was killed. Sometimes a man had to fight wild lions or tigers. The Romans copied these bloody Etruscan combats and made them even more gruesome. These contests were held for hundreds of years. In later times they were staged for the entertainment of the Roman populace in the great amphitheaters which existed in the more important Latin towns, including Rome itself.

THE REPUBLIC

509 B.C. to 27 B.C.

In spite of the teacher-pupil relationship, all was not love and peace between the Romans and the Etruscans, for they would often attack each other. Sometimes one side would win, sometimes the other. Then, in about 600 B.C., the Etruscans won a victory over the Romans, and an Etruscan chieftain moved into Rome and took over as king. For a period of almost a hundred years Rome was ruled by a line of Etruscan kings who were cruel and ruthless. Eventually the Romans revolted against their oppressors, ousting the last Etruscan king, called Tarquin the Proud, in 509 B.C. and setting up a republic.

The Romans were now ready to run their own government. Civilization took a step forward.

In the new Roman republic, the citizens were divided into three classes: the wealthy upper class (patricians), ordinary free citizens (plebeians), and slaves. Only the patricians were allowed to hold office in the government. Two consuls were elected from their own ranks; two or more magistrates were chosen to run the government offices, and an important body of lawmakers, called the Senate, was formed.

The plebeians had to do all the jobs that the patricians shunned. They worked at hard labor on the farms. They served in the ordinary ranks of the Roman army, commanded by patrician officers. The slaves and women were not permitted even to vote. Since there were no written laws, the patricians could take advantage of the people in any way they wished—and could call their practices legal.

Over a period of time, the plebeians began fighting for their rights. They had little success at first, but finally they organized themselves and marched out of the city, threatening to form their own town. This was too much for the patricians, who realized that they would have to perform their own labor and fight in the ranks of the army. At last the plebeians won the right to form their own Assembly and to elect two officers, called tribunes. The tribunes had the option to reject any acts proposed by the patricians that were unfair to the common people by merely calling out the word "Veto," which means "I forbid" in Latin.

For the next fifty years or so, the plebeians fought to have the laws written down so they would not need to trust patrician memories. In 450 B.C., a set of laws called the "Law of the Twelve Tables" was published, becoming the basis for all Roman law. This supposedly gave the ordinary people an equal chance for justice.

Within the next century, the conflict between classes diminished. Some of the plebeians were becoming rich from trading, and many patricians were becoming poorer. Some patricians could no longer afford to keep large numbers of slaves, so they had to free some of them. Many slaves were artisans in various crafts; others were traders. The freed slaves were still not allowed to vote or hold office, but they were able to engage in business, and a few grew wealthy. The newly rich plebeians, however, could now hold office, and some among them even became senators.

Now the rich men of all classes—patricians, plebeians, and former slaves—banded together against the poor. The laws made to protect the poor were largely disregarded. From time to time, leaders arose to defend individual rights of the people, especially the rights of returned soldiers, but one after another such leaders were assassinated.

By this time, the Romans had been exposed to the Greeks who came to trade with them. From them the Romans learned the Greek alphabet, which enabled them to write down their business transactions. Money had now become the medium of exchange, replacing the barter system which had been used for centuries. The Romans also learned the Greek systems of coins, measures, and weights, and applied them in their trading. The Romans even adopted the gods and heroes of the Greeks, changing their names but not the myths or legends about them. The Greek god Zeus became Jupiter; Ares was Mars; Aphrodite became Venus; Poseidon, Neptune; Heracles, the Greek strongman, was called Hercules; Odysseus, the Greek adventurer, became Ulysses; Apollo, the sun-god, remained Apollo.

Rome's Rise to Power

The ousting of the Etruscan kings in 509 B.C. had not ended the invasions of Rome by the Etruscans, or vice versa. Neither did it stop the Etruscan fleets from carrying on trade with Mediterranean countries. It took at least another two hundred years of battles for Rome to finally defeat its neighbors.

In the meantime, Etruria began to go into a decline after being defeated by other powers. In 474 B.C. the Etruscans suffered a great defeat at sea, losing many of their ships and sailors in a battle with the Greek city-state Syracuse, in Sicily. About a hundred years later, in 396 B.C., the Romans captured the city of Veii, an Etruscan stronghold, and this further weakened Etruria. A few years later, in 390 B.C., a heavy invasion of Gauls from the north visited great destruction on all of Etruria. This series of events led to the collapse of the land and sea power of the Etruscans.

Rome, however, did not escape the raids of the Gauls. As the invaders carried their raids south down the Italian peninsula, Rome was sacked, burned, and almost destroyed. But by that time, the Gauls had suffered a heavy loss of their soldiers from disease and hunger. This put the Romans in a position to buy off the leader of the Gauls with a heavy payment of gold. After receiving this tribute, the Gauls left Rome.

The devastation of Rome did not defeat the Roman spirit but rather seems to have given the people new energy. For a century the Romans rebuilt their city and proceeded with a series of conquests to establish Rome as the head of all the Latin towns. By 290 B.C., Rome ruled all of central Italy, having vanquished the Etruscans completely. Roman territories reached from the Arno River on the north to the Grecian colonies on the south. Along the Arno River, which bordered the homeland of the Gauls, the Romans built a line of defense in the form of garrisons and colonial cities, which prevented the Gauls from attacking Rome again.

The Romans conquered more territory and set up a series of vassal states which looked to them for leadership and paid taxes to them. The Romans expanded their trade in farm produce, leather goods, and other products, prospering to the point where they began to search out opportunities for even greater gains. Now Rome was on the verge of becoming an international power, but the city-state of Carthage was a powerful competitor. This North African trading center had ruled the Mediterranean for about five hundred years, since Phoenician days. It had a large fleet of ships, many colonies, and great wealth. Rome wanted Carthage out of the way, and Carthage strongly resented Rome's competition on the seas. They were headed toward war.

The First Punic War

The year 264 B.C. marked the beginning of three wars between Rome and Carthage. They are called the Punic Wars, from the word *Punicus,* which means Phoenician in Latin. (The Phoenicians founded Carthage in about the 9th century B.C.)

The First Punic War lasted twenty-five years, with great losses of men and ships on both sides. It began in Sicily, which had been colonized by both Greeks and Carthaginians. Two cities, Syracuse and Messana, were fighting each other. Carthage sent an army to aid Syracuse, and Rome sent soldiers to assist Messana. After a number of bitter battles, the Romans defeated the Carthaginians and drove them out of most of Sicily. But this did not finish the war. Carthage still had command of the seas. In order for Rome to hold control of Sicily, the Romans would be forced to fight Carthage at sea.

The Carthaginians were master shipbuilders and sea-farers. The Romans, on the other hand, had very little knowledge of ships and fighting on the seas. However, they managed to capture a Carthaginian ship. Using it as a model, they built a fleet of similar vessels. The ships were propelled by oars, so the Romans had to train some of their men to be oarsmen. After that, the Romans were ready to engage in sea battles with the Carthaginians.

When fighting at sea, the Carthaginians would ram an enemy ship repeatedly until they could overturn it. But with their engineering skills the Romans created a new invention, the *corvus*. This was a plank of wood held up-right against a mast by means of a ring and pulley. A long, sharp spike was fixed at the front of the board. When the Romans rammed a vessel, they dropped the board onto the enemy ship; the spike dug deeply into the deck, and the board formed a bridge between the two ships. Then the Romans would rush across with drawn swords to fight the enemy in hand-to-hand combat, at which they were usually successful.

Nevertheless, during twenty-five years of fighting, both sides suffered tremendous losses. At last, in 239 B.C., a great victory was won by the Romans. Carthage was forced to relinquish all its possessions in Sicily and to pay huge sums of money in reparations to Rome.

The Second Punic War

In 218 B.C., the Second Punic War began, bringing on seventeen more years of hostilities between Rome and Carthage.

Prior to this time, the Roman armies had consisted of a motley group of farmers, sheepherders, and common citizens who provided their own clothing and weapons and were paid with a share of the plunder. But now Rome had a professional army outfitted with armor, helmets, and an assortment of weapons, including spears, javelins, and swords. The soldiers enlisted for a period of twenty years and were paid a salary. Part of their pay was in salt, a precious commodity at that time. (The word salary comes from *sal,* the Latin word for salt.) These new professional soldiers were called the Roman legions.

During this period, Carthage had an army in Spain, led by one of the greatest generals in history, Hannibal. Hannibal's father, Hamilcar Barca, a great Carthaginian general in the First Punic War, bore a raging hatred against Rome. When Hannibal was only eleven years old, his father made him vow to conquer the Romans when he grew up. Hamilcar became governor of the Carthaginian

Roman soldier

Roman shield

Roman helmets

part of Spain, planning to use this as a base for a land attack on Italy.

When Hannibal was twenty-six years old his father died. True to his vow, Hannibal organized his troops and set out from Spain to invade Italy. In order to do this, he had to perform an unbelievably difficult feat. Taking fifty thousand foot soldiers, nine thousand horsemen, a number of huge baggage wagons, and thirty-seven heavy battle elephants, he proceeded to cross first the Pyrenees mountains and then the Alps. The army had to travel on narrow, twisting mountain roads, in all kinds of winter weather, under the greatest hardships. Hannibal won the loyalty of his troops by being one of them—he slept on the ground with them, ate with them, and trudged the roads with them.

Although it is almost impossible to believe that he accomplished this task, Hannibal and a large part of his army, even including some of the elephants, actually succeeded in reaching Italy.

For two years, Hannibal and his army ravaged the Italian countryside and plundered the villages. Finally, Hannibal had to face the Roman legions at the town of Cannae, near Rome. Hannibal's soldiers fought ferociously and visited a great defeat on the Romans. By now, however, the Carthaginian forces had become depleted through disease and battle, and Hannibal was not able to muster an attack on Rome itself, which was surrounded by a formidable wall. He therefore led his army back into the mountains and continued to make raids on the countryside.

Some time after the battle at Cannae, the Romans invaded Spain and fought the Carthaginians there. The troops were led by a young Roman patrician, Publius Cornelius Scipio, who distinguished himself by defeating the enemy, laying the foundation for turning Spain into a Roman province. Because of his success in Europe, he was ordered to invade Africa and fight the Carthaginians there. The Roman legions under his command devastated the lands around Carthage, just as Hannibal had pillaged the villages around Rome.

In desperation Carthage sent a message to Hannibal, ordering him to return to Africa with his army to fight the Romans and stop them before they destroyed the city of Carthage itself. A great battle between the Roman legions and Hannibal's army ensued at the village of Zama, about eighty miles from Carthage. Hannibal's army put up a valiant fight but was defeated.

In 201 B.C., Carthage was forced to surrender, and the Second Punic War came to an end. Rather than allow the Romans to take him prisoner, Hannibal drank poison and died.

At the end of the Second Punic War, Carthage had to give up all its colonies, and many of its citizens became slaves in Rome. Nevertheless, the city of Carthage still stood, and some Roman leaders believed strongly that Carthage continued to be a threat to Rome. Cato, a Roman senator, wanted to see the city completely wiped out. At every session of the Senate, he would call out, "Carthage must be destroyed."

The Third Punic War

Cato's wish eventually came true. In 149 B.C. the Romans provoked a Third Punic War.

Carthage, in spite of all its setbacks, continued to trade and prosper. Although Carthage no longer actually competed with Rome, its prosperity aroused the envy of the powerful Romans, who resented any wealth in the world but their own. Rome persuaded the Numidians, neighbors of Carthage, to encroach upon the city. The Carthaginians were forced to fight to defend themselves. The Romans claimed that this was a violation of the treaty by which Carthage was not allowed to make war without the permission of Rome. Now they made ridiculous demands on Carthage. Primarily, they ordered that the people desert the city of Carthage and move to a place at least ten miles from the sea. This was an impossible demand to fulfill, inasmuch as the people of Carthage were wholly dependent on the sea for their trade. The Carthaginians prepared to resist, which gave the Romans an excuse to attack them.

For three years the Romans pounded at the heavy walls

of the city with huge battering rams. In the meantime, they built a stone breakwater around Carthage's outer harbor, so that no ships could enter or leave. Unable to get food, the inhabitants were starving; nevertheless, they were determined to hold out as long as the city stood.

Finally, the Romans broke through the walls of Carthage and rushed into the city, killing thousands of people and taking about fifty thousand as slaves. As a final touch, they burned the city to the ground and plowed it under, pouring salt into the furrows so that nothing could ever grow there again. Thus the Third Punic War ended, with the Romans again victorious.

After the Punic Wars

What did the Romans gain by all these successful wars? For one thing, they learned how to build warships and how to use them. Now Rome could send forces to Africa, Spain, Greece, and the Middle East. It not only was able to set up trade alliances, but managed to bring many countries under Roman rule, exacting heavy payments from them.

By the time the republic had existed for about 300 years, Rome had added Sicily, Sardinia, Corsica, and the South of Spain to its possessions. Then parts of Asia Minor, Greece, and Macedonia were conquered.

The visits of the Roman legions to these countries were not altogether destructive, however. The legions spread the Latin language throughout the western world. They built roads, bridges, and aqueducts, the remains of which can still be seen today. In many countries typical Roman towns were set up—in some places, only a simple group of buildings made of brick and timber, where a colony of military veterans settled; in others, luxurious buildings with marble colonnades, used for the local government offices.

The layouts of the towns all followed the same general Roman pattern. In the center was a large open space called the forum. Here business people gathered to carry on trade. The temple stood in a prominent place in the forum. Statues were set up all around. The streets nearby were occupied by a variety of shops. Every town had its Roman bathhouses where men could spend whole afternoons taking relaxing sweats and massages. Then they might meet in cooling rooms to conduct business or just to discuss the news and gossip of the day.

By about 100 B.C., fifty years after the final conquest of Carthage, Rome was the wealthiest and most powerful nation in the world. The rich patricians turned away from their comparatively simple style of living and surrounded themselves with the utmost in luxury. Some had thousands of slaves to farm their huge estates. They also had many slaves to wait upon them in their villas and mansions as barbers, masseurs, personal maids, hairdressers, and various other kinds of attendants. Slaves were cooks and waiters, preparing and serving the finest imported foods and

Coins depicting Roman emperors

wines to their masters and their guests, who reclined on couches while they dined. For the entertainment of the patricians, talented slaves performed dances and played musical instruments.

These rich men and women wore garments of luxurious silks, linens, and wools. Their homes had beautiful gardens adorned with fine statues. They assembled private libraries of books written on papyrus scrolls. The educated Greek slaves served as teachers for the Romans' children.

In strange contrast to the more civilized activities, there were the violent and brutal gladiatorial fights. Each city had its amphitheater where these gruesome spectacles had become a very popular form of entertainment.

How did this great prosperity affect the disadvantaged? They fared very badly, partly because the rights which previous generations had gained for the poor were mostly disregarded by the wealthy senators and other Romans. Upon returning home after years of service, the farmers who had fought for Rome found their land overgrown with weeds and the soil depleted. Even if they managed to reclaim the land, they could not sell their produce at prices low enough to compete with slave labor. Unable to pay their debts or taxes, many lost their land altogether.

When their livelihood on the land was ruined, most of the farmers moved into Rome or other Roman towns. There they found mobs of unemployed people like themselves. They formed a large slum population which received only a dole of grain for food. They lived a life of despair. To forget their hunger and misery, they attended the gladiatorial contests and chariot races. Admission was free, because tickets were given away by politicians to win favor with the voters.

As the division between rich and poor widened, there were violent riots in the streets of Rome. To add to this disorder, the people in other Italian towns revolted. They objected to being heavily taxed by men whom they had no part in electing. They demanded full Roman citizenship with all its rights. The Italian cities formed their own state and named it "Italica." They started an uprising against Rome, called the "Social War," lasting from 90 to 88 B.C. There were heavy losses on both sides, neither gaining a definite victory. But finally the cities were once again part of Rome, and the people were granted full citizenship.

The end of the Social War, however, did not bring peace to Rome. Several military leaders who had acquired fame in the Roman adventures of conquest had gained followers of their own. Each general wanted to rule Rome, and there were several wars between the contenders. In about 80 B.C., a general named Sulla marched into Rome with his legions and seized the city.

THE ROMAN DICTATORS

80 B.C. to 27 B.C.

Sulla became the first Roman dictator—the sole and supreme ruler of all the Roman provinces. His first act was to order the execution of citizens suspected of democratic sympathies. He made daily lists of people to be killed. He enforced the rights of the rich over the poor, putting all authority into the hands of the wealthy senators and reducing the hard-won power of the Assembly and the tribunes. Sulla ruled with an iron hand, enriching himself in his position. At the end of four years he retired, to devote the rest of his life to his own pleasures.

By about 60 B.C., the great and famous general Julius Caesar had conquered most of Gaul (present-day France). He had also successfully invaded the coast of Britain and parts of Germany. Flushed with success, he aspired to become dictator of Rome. However, two other distinguished generals had the same ambition. One was Pompey, who had conquered Jerusalem and large parts of Asia Minor and had fought with great success in Spain. The other was Crassus, who had defeated the army of Spartacus, a former slave who had led a bloody revolt. Each general had his own followers—loyal members of his troops as well as citizen supporters—yet no one of the three potential dictators was able to gain a majority of followers. Therefore the three decided to share the powers of government and to rule Rome together. Historians refer to this as "The First Triumvirate."

The three-man rule did not last long, however. Pompey and Crassus each set out to seek further military glories. Crassus led his troops to Asia Minor and shortly afterward was killed in battle.

In the meantime, Pompey established an extra army in Spain under the leadership of some of his officers. Having accomplished this, Pompey led his own army to Greece.

Caesar surprised and defeated Pompey's army in Spain. Then he met Pompey in Greece and overcame his army there in a decisive battle. Pompey tried to escape by fleeing to Egypt, but Caesar followed him and found out when he arrived that Pompey had been murdered by a follower of the twelve-year-old Egyptian king, Ptolemy XII.

Now Caesar seemed to have the power of Rome entirely in his own hands, but his arrival in Alexandria prompted an attack on his camp by the Egyptian soldiers and by the Roman troops which had remained faithful to Pompey. He returned the attack, drove the soldiers into the Nile, and drowned Ptolemy. The Egyptian fleet was in the harbor at Alexandria, and Caesar's men succeeded in setting fire to the ships. Sparks from the burning fleet fell on the famous library at Alexandria, destroying it and all its treasured papyrus books.

The power was now indeed Caesar's. He set up a new Egyptian government under Roman rule. He put Cleopatra, Ptolemy's 21-year-old sister, on the throne and promptly fell in love with her.

Instead of returning to Rome to attend to his duties, Caesar spent a whole year in Egypt with Cleopatra. When he finally did return to Rome, he brought Cleopatra with him. The obvious influence of this young queen over Caesar, who was then in his late fifties, created tremendous resentment among the Roman people. In spite of the ill feeling, however, in 46 B.C., Caesar was given the position of sole dictator for ten years, and only a year later, he was made dictator for life.

Caesar made serious efforts to improve the Roman government. He reformed the administration of the distant provinces and gave their inhabitants the rights of citizenship. He permitted freed slaves to become members of the Senate, and he proposed laws for the good of the common people. These liberal laws of course made Caesar unpopular with the wealthy men who held the most power in the state.

Caesar was afflicted with great personal vanity. Under the influence of Cleopatra, he had become imbued with the idea of being a god-king, according to the custom of the Egyptian rulers. Once, at the public games, his close friend Mark Antony offered Caesar a crown. For the benefit of the crowd Caesar made a great gesture of refusing it. But he had already adopted the robe, throne,

71

and ivory scepter, such as had been used by the early kings of Rome, and was depicted as a god on coins and statues.

In the procession opening the athletic games, Caesar's image was paraded in the arena, together with those of the Roman gods, and his statue, inscribed with the words "To the unconquerable god!" was set up in a temple.

With supreme confidence in himself, Caesar disregarded the laws of the republic and ruled the cities and provinces as a one-man government. His domineering methods and godlike pretensions made him a host of enemies. The great Roman orator Cicero spoke out against Caesar in beautifully written speeches that aroused the public. Soon even Caesar's closest supporters turned against him, and a conspiracy was hatched, led by Caesar's friend Brutus. On the Ides of March (the fifteenth) in 44 B.C., Caesar was attacked in the Senate and stabbed twenty-three times.

Mark Antony and some of his soldiers hunted down the assassins and killed them. Then Antony seized power and formed a three-way dictatorship with Octavian, Caesar's adopted son and heir, and a wealthy patrician named Lepidus. Octavian was to rule Rome and the provinces of the West; Mark Antony would rule Egypt and the East; Lepidus would have charge of Carthaginian Africa.

No sooner had Antony reached Egypt than he fell under the spell of Cleopatra, as Caesar had done before him. He gave himself up to amusements in the company of

Cleopatra, and the idea of making himself a god-king took over his mind as it had Caesar's.

Octavian in Rome was greatly opposed to Antony's behavior with Cleopatra in Egypt. For one thing, Antony was divorcing his wife, who happened to be Octavian's own sister, and planning to marry Cleopatra. For another, Octavian was displeased with Antony's neglect of his duties. Octavian appealed to the Senate and persuaded it to remove Antony from his dictatorship. Then he sailed off with his navy to launch an attack on Antony's and Cleopatra's ships. In 31 B.C., Octavian attacked the Egyptian fleet in a great sea battle at Actium, off the northwest coast of Greece, winning a decisive victory. Antony and Cleopatra deserted the ships and escaped to Alexandria, but Octavian's forces overtook them there. In despair over his defeat, Antony stabbed himself to death.

Cleopatra's next move was to try to win over Octavian, just as she had previously enchanted both Caesar and Antony. But Octavian refused to succumb to her wiles and proceeded to conquer Egypt, making it a Roman province in 30 B.C. Cleopatra, despondent over the loss of her country, placed a poison asp to her breast and allowed it to bite her. Her death marked the end of the Ptolemies as the rulers of Egypt.

Now Octavian found himself master of the whole Roman world. This marked the beginning of the end of the republic and the approach of the first stage of the Roman Empire.

THE ROMAN EMPIRE

27 B.C. to A.D. 476

After defeating Antony and Cleopatra, Octavian returned to Rome, where he was greeted by a cheering multitude. Shortly afterward, in 27 B.C., the Senate gave him the title *Imperator,* meaning "emperor." They also gave him a new name, *Augustus,* "revered one." Augustus claimed that he did not wish to be a king or dictator, but rather planned only to carry out the wishes of the people through the power of the Senate. At first he retained the form of the republic, but gradually he assumed more and more personal power, and eventually ruled as dictator and emperor of the whole Roman world, until his death in A.D. 14.

Augustus contributed considerably to the strength and reputation of Rome. The finances of the state were organized on a more efficient basis, and business was encouraged by the government. Large sums of money were spent on erecting beautiful buildings, including a new Senate building. Augustus is said to have remarked, "I found Rome brick and left it marble."

The time of Augustus' reign is known as "The Golden

Roman empress

Roman crowns

Age of Roman Literature." Over the preceding three hundred years, Roman culture had greatly advanced. Augustus encouraged the growth of literature and surrounded himself with talented writers. Virgil wrote the *Aeneid,* an epic poem in the manner of Homer which described the adventures of Aeneas, the Trojan warrior whom the Romans credited with founding the Latin race. Ovid wrote songs and poems of great beauty; a complete history of Rome up to that time was written by Livy; and a 37-volume *Natural History* written by Pliny brought the scientific knowledge of the Greeks to the Roman world.

During the reign of Augustus, Jesus was born in the Eastern territory that was under Roman rule. But it was not until a number of years after Augustus' death that the teachings of Christianity were introduced into Rome by the disciples Paul and Peter. Both were executed for spreading the Christian teachings, but nevertheless Christianity became known throughout the Roman world. In keeping with their religious belief, the Christians refused to worship the old Roman gods or to honor the emperors as gods. Consequently, during the next three hundred years the Christians were persecuted in a barbarous manner.

Over a period of more than four hundred years, following Augustus, eighty-four different emperors ruled all or part of the Roman Empire. Some reigned for only a few weeks or months and then were murdered by ambitious men who managed to usurp the throne. Only a few of them were important to history, either for good or evil.

The four emperors after Augustus were all related to Julius Caesar by either birth or adoption. The first of the four, Tiberius, ruled from A.D. 14 to 37. He reorganized the finances of the state, and Rome remained prosperous during his reign. However, he became unpopular because of his personal vices and cruelties. He was extremely suspicious of the members of his court and had them murdered on the slightest pretext.

Caligula, a demented monster, succeeded Tiberius and reigned from A.D. 37 to 41. He performed senseless cruelties and enacted incredibly weird rulings. He is said to have regretted that "all people do not have a single neck to be severed with one blow." At one point, Caligula is thought to have appointed his horse consul. Caligula had reigned for only four years when he was murdered.

When Caligula was killed, his uncle Claudius was found hiding behind a curtain. The soldiers dragged him out and made him emperor. Claudius reigned from A.D. 41 to 54. His principal accomplishment was conquering the southern part of Britain and making it a Roman province. His fourth wife, his niece Agrippina, influenced Claudius to name her son Nero as his successor, instead of his own son. Having succeeded in this, she had Claudius poisoned in order to hasten Nero's accession.

Nero gained the throne in A.D. 54. He was a vain, cruel, and probably insane man who fancied himself a great poet and musician. His reign of fourteen years was filled with terror. He initiated the mass persecutions of the Christians, thousands of whom were thrown to the lions and tigers in the arena, or were burned alive or put to death in other savage ways. He murdered both his mother and his wife for petty reasons.

Nero became decidedly unpopular in Rome, and when the Roman legions suffered a great defeat in Britain, the people became defiant. Then the Roman forces in Spain rose in an insurrection led by a general named Galba. In A.D. 68, as Galba and his troops advanced upon Rome, Nero lost all hope of retaining his throne and committed suicide. Galba seized the throne and became emperor.

Beginning with Galba, Rome had four emperors in one year. The first three were murdered one by one after a few months' reign. The fourth one, Vespasian, ruled from A.D. 69 to 79.

Before becoming emperor, Vespasian was a Roman general in charge of trying to put down a revolt in Jerusalem. The Jewish inhabitants, who had been greatly oppressed by the Romans for about a hundred years, rose up against the government. Vespasian and his legions fought the rebels for several years, but were unable to overcome the uprising. Finally, Vespasian turned over the fight to his son Titus. In A.D. 70, Titus ordered the destruction of Jerusalem. The Jews were taken as slaves and dispersed throughout the Mediterranean world.

As a reward for his success in Jerusalem, in A.D. 71, Titus was made co-ruler with Vespasian. Upon his father's death in A.D. 79, Titus became sole ruler, reigning until A.D. 81. In Rome, Titus was notable as a builder. Among

Ruins of ancient Coliseum

his outstanding accomplishments was the completion of the famous Coliseum and a giant bathhouse.

Titus was succeeded by his brother Domitian, who ruled from A.D. 81 to 96. He was obsessed by the concept of "law and order" and inflicted many cruel punishments in its name, becoming a greatly hated despot. Finally, after he had ruled for fifteen years, his wife conspired to have him murdered.

The Second and Third Centuries A.D.

In contrast to the insanity and violence of the first century of the empire, the second century gave Rome its most prosperous years, under four capable rulers.

The first was Trajan, a military commander born in Spain, who ruled from A.D. 98 to 117. He extended the Roman territories to the maximum, annexing Armenia, Assyria, Mesopotamia and the Sinai Peninsula. Rome was now the center of a widespread empire in Europe, Africa, and the Middle East.

Except for the slaves, all the inhabitants of this monumental empire were Roman citizens protected by Roman law. They were allowed, however, to speak their own languages and worship their own gods.

At this time, all the Roman possessions in Europe were surrounded by fierce Germanic tribes—the Franks, the Vandals, the Alemanni, the Visigoths (West Goths) and the Ostrogoths (East Goths). At various times the Roman legions stationed at the many border points engaged in battle with these barbarians. Sometimes the untrained savage tribes were victorious, but usually the strictly disciplined legions won.

Trajan chose as his successor Hadrian, also a Spaniard and a military man, who ruled from A.D. 117 to 138. Fearful of the ever-growing danger of the barbarian invasions, Hadrian decided to reduce Roman territory. He abandoned the conquests made by Trajan and also dispensed with North Britain. To protect the Britons from invasion by the dangerous Scots and Picts, he built the famous Hadrian's Wall across Britain. He also built several protective walls in Germany. Hadrian traveled widely about the Roman possessions, beautifying cities with new architecture and putting their governments in order.

During Hadrian's reign, in A.D. 132, there was again a revolt in Jerusalem against the oppressive Roman rule. Hadrian's legions destroyed the city totally, including the Jewish temple, which they replaced with a temple to Jupiter. All Jews were forbidden to enter Jerusalem, and a second and even greater dispersion took place, scattering the people throughout the Roman world.

To succeed him, Hadrian named his adopted heir, Antoninus. He was a good administrator, and Rome prospered under his rule, from A.D. 138 to 161.

In A.D. 161 Antoninus' adopted son Marcus Aurelius succeeded to the throne. He was a renowned writer and philosopher as well as a capable emperor. In spite of poor health, Marcus Aurelius held the social order together through a series of bad years—years of failing crops and famines, great floods, raids by the barbarians, revolts in the provinces and finally a terrible pestilence. He worked hard for long hours at a time, concerning himself with practically every public problem. He tried to limit the gladiatorial contests, to elevate public morals, and to see that roads were maintained, among many other matters.

During the prosperous second century A.D., the wealthy Romans were better educated and more cultured than their ancestors. They still indulged in all forms of luxury, but on a more refined scale. The greatest delicacies and ornaments were imported from distant lands. Valuable furs and gems, Oriental carpets, rare spices and wines were brought from Arabia, India, China, Persia, and other exotic places. The wealthy had no special interest in

science and literature, but they acquired elaborate libraries of books written on papyrus scrolls, which few of them
read. When not attending to business, most rich Romans
were content to feast, adorn themselves and their homes,
loll in the baths, and watch the circuses, the bawdy theatri-
cal performances, or the deadly games in the Coliseum.

The common people and the slaves, on the other hand,

Kitchen utensils from Pompeii

led miserable lives, with no hope for anything better. Consequently many of them became attracted to the Christian religion, with its promise of salvation and a better afterlife in heaven.

In the third century, the empire slowly began to split into two parts. In A.D. 284, Diocletian became emperor. He moved his headquarters to Nicomedia, a city in Asia Minor. To keep track of affairs in Italy, he appointed Maximian as a second and equal emperor, with headquarters at Milan. They worked together, both of them signing all decrees. During this double reign, Britain was restored to the empire. Invasion by the Persians was resisted, and some of the barbarians were driven out of Italy. But there was severe persecution of the Christians, and certain economic measures were unsuccessful. Great differences developed between the two emperors, and much dissension arose among the people. In A.D. 305, both emperors abdicated. Diocletian retired to a luxurious castle at Salona, on the Adriatic Sea.

Following the abdications, Galerius became emperor in the east, and Severus was emperor in the west. Upon the death of Galerius in 310, there were four contenders for the throne. Constantine and Licinius overwhelmed the other two in battle, and in A.D. 311 they became co-emperors.

Constantine ruled the western part of the empire; Licinius had power over the eastern part. Seeing the barbarian invasions as a growing threat, they decided that the Roman Empire needed a single idea to unite the people. Christianity had by that time taken hold of the minds of thousands of the common people and slaves. Why not use the new religion as a unifying bond among the inhabitants? Constantine and Licinius issued a joint edict favoring toleration of the Christians. This ended the persecutions which had gone on for over three hundred years. But it was too late for Roman unity.

Constantine and Licinius were not always united in their ideas, and quarrels arose which led to war between them. Licinius was soon killed in battle, and Constantine became the sole ruler of the Roman Empire in A.D. 324. He moved the Roman capital to Byzantium, the site of present-day Istanbul. The city had been founded by the Greeks a thousand years earlier but had become one of the Roman conquests.

Constantine summoned architects, engineers, and builders to construct a brand-new city more luxurious than Rome itself. Within six years, the new city was completed, a model of beautiful architecture, decorated with art and treasures from every part of the Roman Empire. The city was located on the Bosporus, a strait connecting the Black Sea and the Sea of Marmara at the crossroads of trade routes between Asia and eastern Europe. He named the city Constantinople, meaning "Constantine's city."

Because he had become more and more interested in the Christian religion, Constantine established the new

Roman capital as a Christian city. But he himself did not embrace the faith until many years later. Constantine had chosen well the location of the new city, for it became a highly successful trading center and brought great wealth to the Byzantines.

Constantine died in A.D. 337. On his deathbed he was baptized a Christian. After his death, the empire was again divided between east and west and remained so for more than half a century. In 394 there was once more a single ruler, Theodosius. He died the next year, and the empire was permanently divided into two separate states—the Western Roman Empire and the Eastern Roman Empire.

DEATH OF THE WESTERN ROMAN EMPIRE

In the fourth and fifth centuries, some barbaric tribes overran more and more of the lands the Romans had controlled. The Visigoths plundered Gaul and Spain, and the Angles, Saxons, and Jutes crossed from northern Germany and Scandinavia into Britain. Then the savage Huns from Asia invaded Italy under their brutish leader Attila. They plundered everything in sight, leaving villages and cities in ruins. It was fortunate for Rome that Attila died during the Italian invasion, for when the Huns lost their leader, they lost their fighting spirit. They marched out of Italy in despair.

However, other barbarian invasions went on. In 455 the Vandals sacked Rome. Then the Visigoths moved south into Italy, and in 475 their leader, Odoacer, overcame the last Roman emperor, Romulus Augustus, and pushed him from the throne. In 476 he became ruler of the western Roman possessions, marking the fall of the Roman Empire.

By now, the city of Rome was in a desperate condition of neglect. The great palaces and public buildings were masses of rubble. The roads had been broken up, the bridges demolished, the schools sent up in flames. The remaining villas of the wealthy were occupied by unwashed barbarians. The civilization which the Sumerians, Egyptians, Greeks and Romans had been building for thousands of years was on its way to oblivion in the western world.

THE EASTERN ROMAN EMPIRE

After the fall of the Western Roman Empire, the Eastern Roman Empire continued for almost a thousand years under a long line of emperors in Byzantium. But rather than remaining Roman in outlook, it turned to Greek and eastern cultures. The official language gradually changed from Latin to Greek, and the eastern Christians broke away from the Roman church, establishing their own Greek Orthodox Church.

The outstanding period of the Byzantine Empire came after the fall of Rome itself. In the year A.D. 527 the emperor Justinian I ascended the throne, reigning for thirty-eight years. Justinian liked all the trappings of imperial rule. He wore luxurious silk robes and a crown encrusted with jewels, and insisted that everyone kneel when coming into his presence.

The emperor had a special talent for selecting capable generals. Belisarius, the greatest military leader of Byzantium, recaptured the North African states, including Carthage, and reconquered Italy from the Ostrogoths. By 555 all Italy and the southern parts of Spain were under Justinian's rule. These conquests, however, were lost again by the end of the century.

Justinian was famous for building hundreds of beautiful churches throughout his land. The most fabulous of these was Santa Sophia, the Church of Holy Wisdom, in Constantinople. It was a masterpiece of Byzantine architecture. The nave was surrounded by forty arched windows and was covered by a magnificent central dome 184 feet high and 102 feet in diameter. All the interior surfaces were covered with marble and gold mosaics. When Constantinople was later captured by the Ottoman Turks, Santa Sophia became an Islamic mosque. Today it is used as a museum of Byzantine art.

Justinian is famous for his code of laws, which have influenced the laws of most western nations today. The whole body of Roman laws, consisting of thousands of statutes, edicts, and amendments, was compiled and simplified by a commission of jurists selected by Justinian. In 534 the laws were published in a series of books entitled *The Corpus of Civil Law.* According to Justinian, the laws were based on humanity and common sense.

Included were new laws granting women's rights, and laws giving mothers equal authority with fathers in bringing up children. (In Rome, this had been the father's right alone.) It is believed that Justinian's wife, the Empress Theodora, influenced these laws in favor of women. Justinian had married her against the wishes of the public, which objected because she was an actress of questionable morals. However, she proved worthy of her position as empress. She was a fine administrator and was her husband's valued advisor over a period of twenty years.

In the Justinian Code, the sentence of death was rarely used. A prison term was considered a waste of a person's useful time and was not to be ordered except in extreme cases. Extremely heavy fines which reduced a person to poverty were not regarded as desirable. However, for serious crimes such as murder, robbery, violence, or treason the penalty was the chopping off of a hand or other extremity, which was of course cruel but did at least spare the offender's life. Nevertheless, there were still some public executions of corrupt officials and others who had committed crimes against the empire. Justinian died in the year 565.

All life in Byzantium centered around religion. Festivals, carnivals, theater performances, athletic games—all were dedicated to God. The blessing of the church was sought for everyday activities. When a house was built, its owner asked for God's favor. Fishing vessels were blessed for a good catch and a safe return. And of course weddings, christenings, and funerals were all religious occasions, just as they usually are today. The artistic creations of Byzantium consisted of religious mosaics, frescos, songs, and poems.

However, peace did not reign in the Eastern Roman Empire. During the eleven centuries of its existence, the empire was invaded by the Goths, Huns, Arabs, Vikings, Slavs, Persians, Bulgars, and Turks. Even the Crusaders stopped off on their way from Europe to the Holy Land. In 1204 they invaded Constantinople and looted it of its most valuable art treasures, which are today to be found on display in many parts of the world.

Sometimes, when attackers could not be held off, the Byzantines were forced to buy peace with payments of gold to their invaders. In the last three hundred years of its existence, the empire was repeatedly attacked by the Turks, who were intent on doing away with the Christian faith and building an empire dedicated to the religion of Islam. More and more Byzantine territory had to be given up, until by the beginning of the fifteenth century, only the city of Constantinople and a small area to the north of it remained in Byzantine hands. By then the city, once a metropolis of over a million people, had been reduced to a mere sixty thousand inhabitants.

In 1453 Mehmet II, Sultan of the Ottoman Turks, laid siege to Constantinople. He had planned a whole year for this attack, and it took only six weeks for the city to fall. Riding a white horse, Mehmet entered the city and rode straight to the Church of Wisdom, declaring it a mosque for Islam. At last, after centuries of fighting, Islam ruled the Near East and the Mediterranean areas. The Byzantine Empire was dead.

ANCIENT INFLUENCES ON TODAY'S WORLD

As we have seen, the ancient civilizations of the Middle East rose and fell many times throughout thousands of years. In this book it has been necessary to omit some periods of time and many rulers. The nations and events included, however, give a picture of the most significant civilizations—how they originated, developed, reached their climax, diminished, and died; also how they influenced languages, laws, art, architecture, religion, and literature. The contributions of the ancient civilizations are reflected in many ways in today's world. We are all enriched by our knowledge of their origin.

A FEW OTHER BOOKS
ABOUT ANCIENT CIVILIZATIONS

For Young Readers (Grade 4 and up)

Asimov, Isaac. *The Roman Republic*. Boston: Houghton Mifflin, 1966.

Brooks, Polly, and Nancy Walworth. *When the World Was Rome*. Philadelphia: Lippincott, 1972.

Coolidge, Olivia. *The Golden Days of Greece*. New York: T.Y. Crowell, 1968.

Glubok, Shirley, ed. *Discovering Tut-Ankh-Amen's Tomb*, abridged edition. New York: Macmillan, 1968.

For Junior High, High School, and Adult Readers

Bronowski, Jacob. *The Ascent of Man*. Boston: Little, Brown, 1976.

Clark, Kenneth McKenzie. *Civilisation: A Personal View*. New York: Harper & Row, 1970.

The Last Two Million Years. New York: Reader's Digest Press, 1974.

Van Loon, Hendrik. *The Story of Mankind*, revised edition. New York: Liveright, 1972.

INDEX AND PRONUNCIATION GUIDE

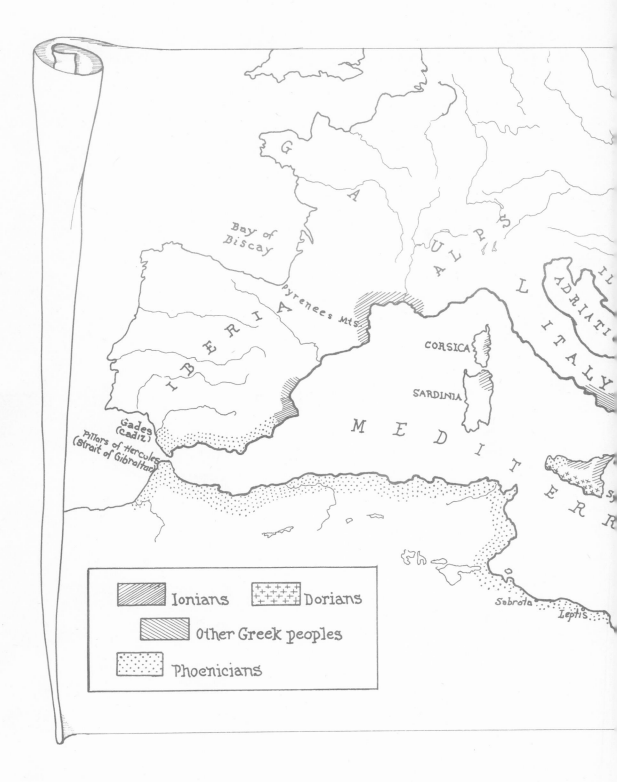

G
A
L

Bay of
Biscay

Pyrenees Mts.

A L P S

I L
A D R I A T I
L I T A L Y

I B E R I A

CORSICA

SARDINIA

Gades
(Cadiz)

Pillars of Hercules
(Strait of Gibraltar)

M E D I T E R R

S

th

Sabrata

Leptis

	Ionians		Dorians
	Other Greek peoples		
	Phoenicians		